Kurelek's Vision
of Canada

William Kurelek sketching, 1964.   Credit: Michel Lambeth

For my friend Sarah,

Kurelek's Vision of Canada

William Kurelek   *Joan Murray*
Joan Murray
14 January '95

Hurtig Publishers
Edmonton

Hurtig Publishers Ltd.
10560-105 Street
Edmonton, Alberta

Canadian Cataloguing in Publication Data

Kurelek, William, 1927–1977.
    Kurelek's vision of Canada

    Bibliography: p.
    ISBN 0-88830-254-1

    1. Kurelek, William, 1927–1977.   2.
Canada in art.   I. Murray, Joan.   II. Title.
ND249.K8A4 1983   759.11   C83-091274-6

Photograph of *B.C. Seen through Sunglasses* by The Downstairs Gallery, Edmonton.
All other paintings photographed by T. E. Moore, Toronto.

Printed and bound in Canada
by D. W. Friesen & Sons

Contents

Acknowledgements

Eight years ago, in Dr. Ben Kanee's home in Vancouver, I saw William Kurelek's painting, *World of Hope* (1965). It was the first time I had noticed the marvellous sense of breadth in Kurelek's landscape, the endless expanse and largeness of vision. Kurelek's work was not seen in public collections like those of the Art Gallery of Ontario or the National Gallery of Canada. It took a Group of Seven collector like Dr. Kanee to show me how superior Kurelek was as a landscape painter.

In later years, I followed Kurelek's exhibitions at the Isaacs Gallery in Toronto with interest, and even met Kurelek himself. I had been planning to interview him for some time when he died in 1977. Before that I had sent students to him from both York University and Scarborough College in Toronto where I lectured on Canadian art in the early 1970s. Kurelek was kind to them. In one case, he even consented to a three-hour videotaped interview. Looking at the tape is a revelation of Kurelek as he was then: nervous, shy, hesitant, honest. In time I wished to interpret the art of the man for myself.

In 1980, I began to research Kurelek's work. In 1982, with the generous assistance of Mutual Life of Canada and the National Museums of Canada, I organized the *Kurelek's Vision of Canada* exhibition for the Robert McLaughlin Gallery in Oshawa, of which I am the director. This book springs from that exhibition which, at time of publication, is still travelling across Canada.

As the exhibition toured Canada, my feelings about Kurelek's landscape subtly changed. I came to recognize Kurelek's handicaps, and his greatness. Kurelek began exhibiting professionally in 1960; the exhibition and this book tell only one side of the story of his work from 1961. Our retrospective look is coherent but not complete in terms of his total *oeuvre*. This is a first word about Kurelek's work, and only about a single aspect of it, not the last. But I hope in one important way it will illustrate the shape of his development.

6

Usually, I enjoy artists' speaking for themselves. I therefore have included excerpts from Kurelek's accounts of his life and art, taken from his extensive writings—his autobiography, *Someone with Me*, his manifestos or forewords to his shows at the Isaacs Gallery, Toronto, the Mira Godard Gallery, Montreal, the Art Gallery of Windsor, and the Art Gallery of Brant, Brantford. Quotations not otherwise identified are on file at the Isaacs Gallery. I am grateful to the Kurelek estate, and particularly to Jean Kurelek, for permission to publish this material. Kurelek's Bible quotations are from the translation by R. A. Knox. The paintings on pages 65, 66, 67, 68, and 69 are from *Who Has Seen the Wind* by W. O. Mitchell, and are reproduced here by permission of the publisher, Macmillan of Canada. The paintings on pages 42, 51, and 54 are from *Kurelek's Canada* by William Kurelek, and are reproduced by permission of the Pagurian Corporation Limited.

Avrom Isaacs, the artist's dealer from the beginning, and his assistant, Martha Black, were extremely helpful in the creation of the list of works to be included in the exhibition and, therefore, in this book. Without their co-operation, I could not have realized this project. Robert Fulford, Barbara Moon, and Maria Tippett have been kind enough to edit my text.

I am grateful for the enthusiastic support given this project by the board of the Robert McLaughlin Gallery. In 1967, through a gift from her husband, C. Ewart McLaughlin, the collection of Alexandra Luke, a member of the group known as Painters Eleven (1953–60), became the core of this gallery's collection. Luke, an early (for Canada) student of Hans Hofmann, the important American abstract painter, was a remarkable, surprising colorist whose work was delicate and vivacious. Within the Oshawa community, she worked practically in isolation. Her immediate circle of friends and acquaintances gave her little support, except that she was allowed to go her own way. Over the years, in the same way, William Kurelek maintained his convictions without compromise. Luke, I am sure, would have respected an exhibition of the work of this artist; she might have sensed a parallel with her own development, and perhaps responded to some of his religious and aesthetic ideals.

The staff of the gallery, as always, provided the assistance required by a project of this magnitude. I wish to thank Margaret Jackson, in particular, who has served as my main assistant on the project, and Bernice Bradt, Patricia Claxton-Oldfield, Garfield Ferguson, Gil Knowler, Jack Leroux, Mary Lee Simcoe, and Theresa Watson. Alexa Liebregts and Debbie White assisted with certain details. Thanks are due also to Jackie Hunter, of The National Gallery of Canada Library, for supplying obscure clippings from the artist's file.

Joan Murray
Director,
The Robert McLaughlin Gallery,
Oshawa, Ontario

7

Picture Making by the Seat of His Pants
Joan Murray

Kurelek was one of the really important landscape painters in Canada but his work, perhaps because of its message, has remained outside the mainstream of Canadian art history. J. Russell Harper mentioned him briefly in *Painting in Canada* (1966); Dennis Reid not at all in *A Concise History of Canadian Painting* (1973). Early critics found his work "sombre," "menacing," "grotesque," and "macabre." His landscapes were "lonely and hostile," they said. There was a "frightening hint of madness" to his work, a sense of lurking terror, chaos and doom—a maniacal quality, as Elizabeth Kilbourn wrote in *Canadian Art* in the early 1960s. All conceded he was unique in Canadian painting.

Among important Canadian artists of recent times, William Kurelek (1927–77) was the only one to believe his ability to make art was literally a gift from God, and must be used in God's service. If this unfashionable conviction set him apart from his contemporaries, so did almost every other circumstance of his creative life, including his attitude to conventional aesthetics and his choice of subject matter. In the midst of Canada's love affair with abstract art, he remained sturdily representational, alternating anecdotal scenes from his prairie boyhood with savagely realistic depictions of the sin and corruption he saw everywhere around him. Far from scorning propaganda, he perceived it as his artistic duty. The winsome documents of immigrant farm life were, as he saw it, the catch-words for his urgent message that Armageddon was at hand. In 1976, at the height of his success, he told a reporter, "I have to stay popular."[1]

And he *was* popular. He was a master of book illustration; in the last four years of his life he either wrote or illustrated fourteen books, twice winning the award for the Best Illustrated Children's Book of the Year from *The New York Times*. When he illustrated Ivan Franko's Ukrainian classic *Fox Mykyta* (published in English in 1978 by Tundra Press), Kurelek identified with Fox Mykyta who, summoned to King Lion to be punished, cleverly outwits the challenger, Wolf the Hungry, and becomes a member of the Royal Council. Curiously, Kurelek's career has a strange similarity to Mykyta's: from his first one-man show in 1960 at the Isaacs Gallery in Toronto, until his untimely death from cancer in 1977 at the age of fifty, he found an enthusiastic and ever-growing group of admirers and collectors; the painter who existed as an outsider in Canadian art created a body of work that has made him today the favourite of a diverse range of people, from the man-on-the-street to Premier Richard Hatfield of New Brunswick.

He was a favourite with the mass media, not only because his paintings told stories and took well to reproduction but because he himself was good copy. He was a Canadian-born Ukrainian farmboy who celebrated his heritage at the very moment that Canadians were congratulating themselves on their multiculturalism. Furthermore, anxious to bring his other message—the religious one—to anyone who would listen, he was searingly candid about his harsh, difficult childhood, his torments as a young adult, his suicide attempts, the four years in a British mental institution, the shock therapy ("fourteen treatments in all...like being executed fourteen times over"[2]) and the redeeming and transforming conversion to Roman Catholicism. By the time he died he was easily the most interviewed and written about of all living Canadian artists.

As a result he risked being dismissed by critics and academics as a mere crowd-pleaser, an author of painted rhetoric, a celebrity illustrator, rather than a serious artist. (And indeed his literalism sometimes evoked unwanted echoes of *Saturday Evening Post* covers.) But contemporary art historians now tend to agree that Kurelek's art transcends his didactic subject matter.

At its best, his work possesses the passionate intensity of a Bosch or a Bruegel. His compositional sense is singular and arresting. His pictorial surfaces are muscular. And there is something else. Kurelek almost never painted landscape as such, but during his lifetime he painted the length and breadth of the country and Canada's physical presence informs almost everything he did. This landscape element, its descriptive power and precision, its authenticity, its use as both compositional armature and conveyor of emotional content, unifies his work—and is the subject of the present collection.

William Kurelek was born in Whitford, Alberta, seventy-five miles northeast of Edmonton. To outsiders, Whitford might look bleak—two grain elevators and three buildings huddled under a vast sky. But to Kurelek, even as a small child, the austere emptiness had its own charm. He responded in the same way to Stonewall, Manitoba, where he moved when he was seven and where his father ran a dairy farm: he loved the "great, free, flat bogland to the east" he said of it.[3]

But his home life was difficult. His father, Metro, was an old-fashioned Ukrainian patriarch (he had come from the village of Borivtsi, in the province of Bukovina) who was harsh and strict, contemptuous of his high-strung, imaginative oldest son. He thought William weak, "not like the other kids." "Wake up and be a boy," Kurelek recalled his father saying one night as he went to sleep. "Don't be a girl."[4] Neither of his parents seemed satisfied with him. And he felt starved for affection.

Painting was the only thing at which he excelled. From Grade One, he knew he was an artist. Encouragement came from the teacher in his one-room school in Stonewall who asked him to do a series of drawings of Canadian history. "It was then that I conceived the idea of some day illustrating the whole of Canadian history," he later recalled.[5] At the same time, a Greek Orthodox priest first aroused his interest in his ethnic heritage.

Kurelek often sat in the kitchen corner after the day's work, listening to his father yarning with the hired hands. His father was a spell-binding spinner of tales; Kurelek dreamed that he himself would someday be such a story-teller. Later, when he moved to a city high school, he envisioned himself surrounded by fellow students listening in admiration to his stories of farm adventures. Instead, he discovered that no one wanted to hear what he had to say. In his paintings, much later, he would find a way to fulfil his dream.

Secretly, Kurelek saw himself as a "shrewd" and "cagey peasant"; however his parents' contempt had already turned him tongue-tied and deeply shy. He was full of baffled pain mingled with fury, arrogance mixed with self-doubt as well as the need for approval. He sought father figures during his entire adult life. In art, the absence of any strong master-craftsman relationship left him dissatisfied with Toronto's Ontario College of Art, which he attended in 1949 and 1950 after graduating from the University of Manitoba with his Bachelor of Arts degree. Hoping to learn from the Mexican Social Realists such as Siqueiros, Orozco, or Diego Rivera, he hitch-hiked to Mexico in 1950, but found no one of sufficient calibre to help him at the school he joined in San Miguel de Allende. He renewed his quest for a mentor in England, after his nervous breakdown and the sojourn in the mental institution. In 1956 and again in 1957 he wrote for an interview to Stanley Spencer, the well-known British figure painter. Spencer never replied. Meanwhile, though, Kurelek had found one satisfactory teacher—in a book. The book was Kimon Nicolaïdes' standard text, *The Natural Way to Draw* (1941), which Kurelek began to devour on his own in Montreal while waiting to sail for Europe. The exercises at the end of each chapter were the making of him as an artist, he said. Nicolaïdes "helped me break into the essence of art as I understand it."[6] Gesture and contour were emphasized in the master's lessons. Kurelek accomplished the whole

Figure 1
Self-Portrait 1957
Watercolour, 45.72 × 35.56 cm
Jean Kurelek, Toronto, Ontario

course, which was supposed to take a year, in three months, using his own body as the model for anatomy assignments and sketching surreptitiously in restaurants and railway stations to master gesture.

The weakness of most of his figurative work—the way in which his figures sometimes seem to have no bones—seems to indicate that, aside from this course, he never drew much from life. He also seems to have been heavily influenced by the way he felt about his subjects. Children, perhaps because his own childhood was grotesque, are always thin, spindly, stick figures.

By the time Kurelek reached England in the mid-1950s, his self-hatred and self-pity had reached a crisis. The outcome was the nervous breakdown of 1957, then hospitalization, and shock therapy. He never stopped painting and produced through this period some remarkable expressions of personal anguish, nightmare phobia, and utter desolation. He titled one canvas *Help Me Please Help Me Please Help Me—Please Help*.

His conversion to the Roman Catholic faith the same year as his breakdown marked the turning point. He returned to Toronto in 1959, and his considerable commercial success can be dated from 1960 with his first one-man show at the Isaacs Gallery. (He was one of the few realists in the Isaacs group of artists, which included Michael Snow, Graham Coughtry, and Gordon Rayner.) Add to this a happily married life and Kurelek finally began feeling that "everything is going my way."[7] He found perhaps even the father he needed in his dealer, Avrom Isaacs. "Tell my father you think my paintings are good," he asked Isaacs on the occasion of his first show.[8]

Kurelek was, both as a person and as a painter, amazed by reality. He responded with wholehearted wonder to the natural world, and this quality appears in his art, making it fresh, direct, and authentic. His work is largely based on first-hand observation. He could paint tellingly the nuances of weather, the bright blue prairie sky (or the sky in its varying moods of darkness or storm), the shiny golden light, and the charm of the spareness and spaciousness of the western landscape.

From the beginning, Kurelek favoured the panorama—a distant, high horizon, a limitless expanse. Man is never lost in the luminous land, but engulfment threatens as he travels from the foreground into the distance, usually on a deliberate, carefully laid out, curving path, as in *Hauling Sheaves to the Threshing Machine* (1961). The dwarfed figure may traverse the featureless whiteness of snow, as in *Winter North of Winnipeg* (1962),

Figure 2
William Kurelek, 1964.
Credit: Michel Lambeth

or the figures—Kurelek himself as a young boy with his family—may confront the night landscape at the end of the journey, as in his 1964 recreation of his family's arrival on their Manitoba farm.

Always, monumental grandeur is inherent in the structure—a sense that the long perspectives meet only somewhere beyond, in infinity. "I work more in world terms," Kurelek once said.[9]

Kurelek had felt no different in his early world—almost overwhelmed by the setting but fascinated by the power of natural forces. Nature was "beautiful but heartless," implacable and often hostile. He'd seen his father's barn burn down, a memory he often recalled later, as in *A Ukrainian Canadian Prairie Tragedy* (1974). Against the panoramic background, the foreground often chronicles suffering, or frantic movement—mourners grieving the death of a child in *Lest We Repent* (1966) or farm workers outpacing a coming storm, as in *Thunder Driven* (1970).

Still, the mood is not always tragic. Just as often, Kurelek strikes a note of awed wonder. "The single outstanding feature of prairie landscape, just as of the ocean, is *expanse*," he wrote in 1970.[10] When in 1974 he painted the Atlantic lobster fisherman looking across the sea to a distant boat, he found himself recalling "the warm glow a prairie farmer gets from seeing a far-off neighbour's farmhouse lights come on in the evenings."[11]

Kurelek brought to his landscape painting both his own sense of doom and his own redemptive rapture. In his heart, he believed a holocaust was inevitable: "... retribution will catch up with us soon."[12] Hence, he used the atomic bomb in the background of some of his works like *Not Going Back to Pick up a Cloak* . . . (1971). "I am not made gloomy by the prospect of the end, by the approaching of nuclear annihilation, by destruction of the world. . . . I am ready for it. It will be a beginning . . . of the salvation of man."[13]

The wind in particular seemed to Kurelek to convey

the breath of God's spirit. In Ireland in 1974, he'd been impressed by the high wind: "The lush valley with the hills...seemed in paroxysm. The trees...were like blown heads of hair."[14] It remained for him a moment of supreme religious insight. Later, the vision of a mystical union with nature came back to him in the form of his own self-portrait, *By The Breath of The Spirit II* (1975). The inspiration came from John 3:8, "the wind breathes where it will, and thou canst hear the sound of it, but knowest nothing of the way it came or the way it goes; so it is, when a man is born by the breath of the Spirit."

By The Breath of The Spirit II is not Kurelek's most accomplished work. It reflects a feature of his paintings at their worst: somehow it lacks focus, or has only a weak centre. However, it also possesses a quality inherent in Kurelek's work at its best: the whole pictorial surface is involved in writhing movement. When this kind of musculature is anchored by a firm composition, the results are fresh and grand. It is this quality that interested artists as disparate as Ivan Eyre and Dennis Burton, Kurelek's peer in the Isaacs group of artists.

Both Eyre and Burton are, of course, western artists. Eyre found that Kurelek was the only painter to depict accurately the prairie landscape, particularly a view down the centre of the fence-lines, which he himself had often studied in the area around his home outside Winnipeg. For Burton, Kurelek's prairie landscape was the only authentic one he knew.

From the beginning, Kurelek painted night scenes. Around 1970 he began to work outside, studying the sky and different kinds of weather. "The most magnificent feature of the prairies is the panorama of the sky, awesomely grand and varied," he wrote in 1975.[15] From high school, he had loved Wordsworth; now in Nature's innocence and beauty, he found God. "Nature of itself is nothing but a blind set of chemical and physical laws.... But it *is* a person, an infinitely wise and powerful De-

signer and Provider who created Nature," he said, and he noted the "beautiful design God put into Nature."[16] "Only a Creator who is beauty itself can create beauty—only those who are made in His image can appreciate that beauty," he said.[17] With beauty, he wished to distract viewers from his moralizing.[18] *Glimmering Tapers 'Round the Day's Dead Sanctities* (1970), in which he depicted the Northern Lights, is perhaps his masterpiece.

Also around 1970 his paintings began to depict fewer western subjects and more of the Ontario countryside or urbanscape. His book *O Toronto*—paintings of, and notes about, the city—was published in 1973 and symbolized his new viewpoint. At the same time, he decided to travel the distance of Canada—to make "the whole country mine."[19] His landscape art was a way of appropriating the country, beautiful and picturesque even when interlaced with evidence of human use.

His difficult personal life, with its wistful searching and its violent transitions, is reflected in the dualism of his work: innocent nostalgia, apocalyptic vision. But many of the more than two thousand paintings he left are unified by the landscape. Kurelek's sense of Canada's physical reality is the most consistent, powerful, and characteristic feature of his work. It is almost as though his native talent had found its own subconscious retort to the wilful subject-orientation of his canvases.

The extraordinary fact of Kurelek's life is that he was so nearly not an artist at all. The forty-eight colour works in this book reveal that, for him, painting was an incredibly difficult activity, and the results were often out of kilter.

Kurelek always carefully documented his sources. He had studied art history at university, and thus had a wide base from which to draw. Though he admired Leonardo, Michelangelo, and Van Gogh, it was the great moralists and illustrators of northern Europe, Bosch and Bruegel, who seized his imagination. Later in his work, he drew

Figure 3
William Kurelek in his basement studio, December 1973.
Credit: Dan Newman, Gamma Photo

inspiration from them, quoting subjects or copying figures. He admired Rouault's *Miserere* series. And he loved American painting. He recalled the work of Thomas Eakins in *Indian Summer on the Humber* (1972). More important were the realists of his own day, like Andrew Wyeth (he had seen a show of his work in Buffalo in the early 1960s and liked his symbolic equivalents of the country, his use of mood and locales).[20] Kurelek liked Edward Hopper, Ben Shahn, and the Canadian Alex Colville. He loved poetry, and drew upon a poem by the English mystical poet Frances Thompson for the titles of the paintings of a show in 1970.

At the Ontario College of Art, he met Graham Coughtry, later one of the artists with whom he showed at the Isaacs Gallery. He was always interested by the work of his peers in the gallery, and not only the realists, like

Jack Chambers, whose *401 Towards London No. 1* (1968-69, Norcen Energy Resources Limited, Toronto) inspired Kurelek's own *Don Valley on a Grey Day* (1972). He also admired the abstract painters in the Isaacs stable, especially those with an interest in landscape, like Gordon Rayner, to whom he wrote a frank fan-letter about his first collage show in 1975: "I really love this show," he wrote (fig. 4). He may have thought of the imagery in Rayner's *The Lamp* (Magnetawan Series) (1964, The Robert McLaughlin Gallery, Oshawa), a glowing blue canvas with a yellow "lamp," or that work's loose painting and largeness of scale, when he painted his own Northern Lights painting. In *Thunder Driven* (1970), the sky looks extraordinarily like a Rayner. (The field itself recalls more an Antoni Tapies.) In *Plane Watchers at Malton* (1972), the freedom of handling of the clouds seems to owe much to Rayner's lessons in pouring paint onto absorbent canvas.

Perhaps the influence of Kurelek's Isaacs Gallery peers can be sensed only in retrospect. From Rayner and others like him in the Isaacs Gallery, he may have assimilated his abstract way of composing and his keen decorative sense. His use of an all-over composition in which every inch was important was common to abstract painters of the day as well as to many folk artists. Kurelek loved Ukrainian vernacular art. He filled his canvases even to the frame (he'd begun with the Isaacs Gallery as a frame-maker, as well as an artist). Sometimes his frames extend the meaning of his canvases. He had a strong sense of central image, around which he discreetly wove his compositions. "I tend to flout artistic rules by doing taboo things like dividing a composition exactly in half," he once said. "I believe aesthetics can take care of themselves."[21] The use of the strong central vertical created a symmetry of design, one which other painters, in particular Ivan Eyre, noticed.

Kurelek had an almost rudimentary sense of composi-

Figure 4
Letter to Gordon Rayner from William Kurelek, March 21,
1975.

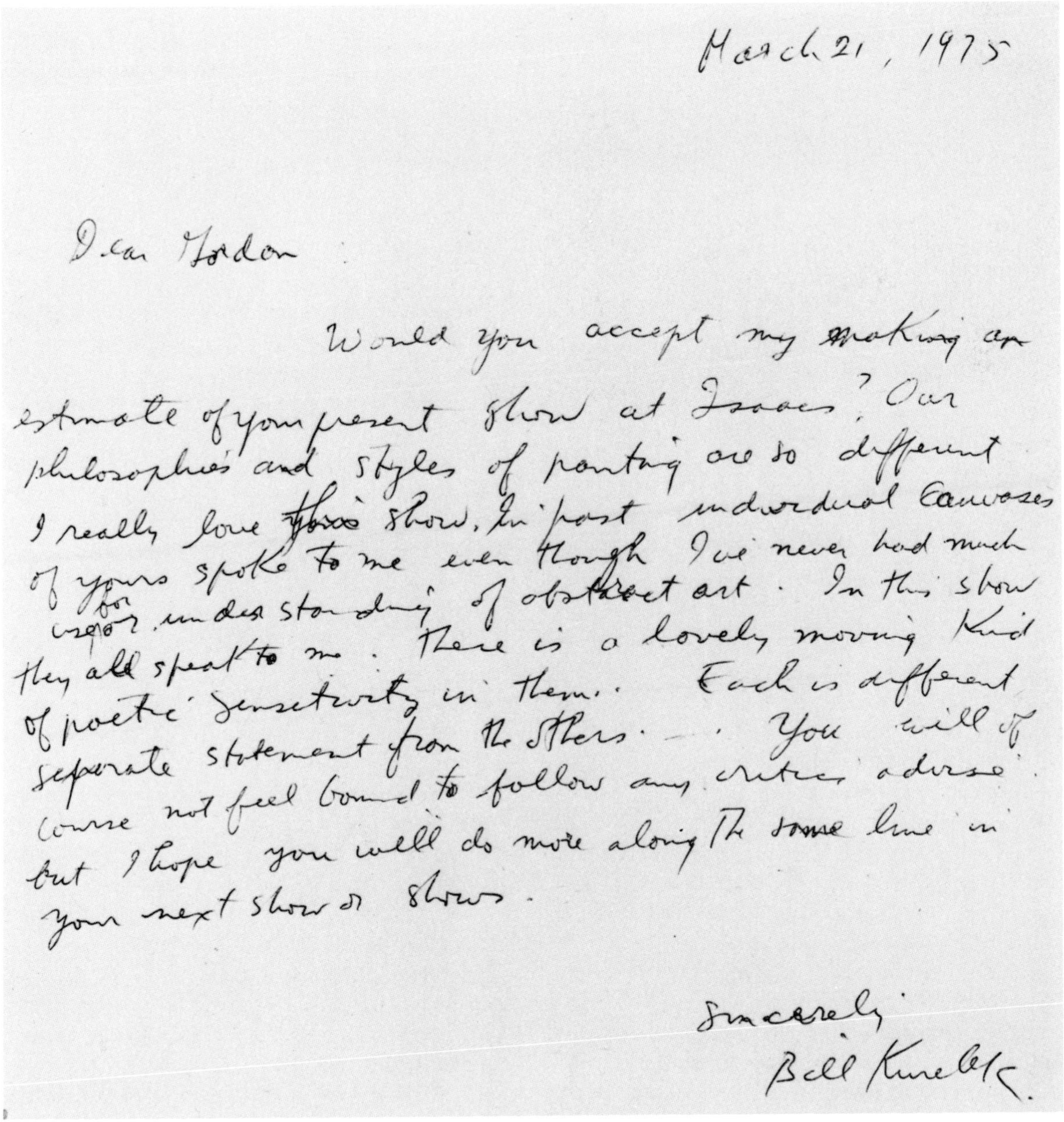

March 21, 1975

Dear Gordon:

Would you accept my making an estimate of your present show at Isaacs? Our philosophies and styles of painting are so different I really love this show. In past individual canvases of yours spoke to me even though I've never had much vigor for understanding of abstract art. In this show they all speak to me. There is a lovely moving kind of poetic sensitivity in them. Each is different separate statement from the others. — You will of course not feel bound to follow any critics advise, but I hope you will do more along the same line in your next show or shows.

Sincerely,
Bill Kurelek.

tion. He saw painting as a way of disposing simple geometric blocks in space. In the earliest work in this book, *Hauling Sheaves to the Threshing Machine* (1961), a haywagon sits in the foreground, a square block over which we must look to seek the expansive landscape, the prairie Kurelek dearly loved. Kurelek's idea of picture making was stark: the land was never more nor less than a flat table top from his earliest work to the paintings he did in 1975 for his book *Fields*. The grass often looks like a mat you can roll up. From an early date in his work, he had tilted the ground plane, often fields in his barren land, towards the picture's surface to exaggerate the distances. But his use of depth could be mechanical. And his usual painting technique was almost preposterously simple and rough: he applied a gesso ground to masonite board, then either oil or acrylic (sometimes in the form of spray), then outlined the composition with a ballpoint pen. For texture, he used coloured pencils; for fine details, he scratched, scrubbed, or brushed the surface. He finished by adding details in pen. This method of fill-in-the-shapes inclined to flat areas. The airbrush helped a little. In *Glimmering Tapers 'Round the Day's Dead Sancti-ties* (1970), he found it useful to express the melting, shimmering screen of the Northern Lights. However, without his spacious vision of the landscape, a two-dimensional surface would invariably have been the result.

Kurelek had other difficulties. His colour sense varied between too garish and too plain. In *The Atheist* (1963), for instance, Cerulean blue—always a difficult colour—is brushed across the top of the canvas to indicate sky. The habit of a solid sky colour remained with him all of his life. For one period in the early 1970s all his barns were the same shade of red. And Kurelek's sense of form was deficient. There is never a doubt that Kurelek's paintings are painful, laborious *constructs*. His bushes sometimes look remarkably like hedgehogs, the expressions on his faces are phony—as in *Pastoral Symphony* (1974)—and his figures are often lumpy, or stick-like. His best figure work, as the illustrations for *Fox Mykyta* prove, are of animals. In the present selection, the best figures are dogs, especially in a 1976 painting used to illustrate a new edition of W. O. Mitchell's classic, *Who Has Seen the Wind*.

Like other artists of his day, Kurelek often used photographs as reference. Much has been made of his camera-like vision. In fact, his paintings are less camera conscious than theatrical. His scenes seem more like dramatic stage-sets in which figures act out a preordained narrative.

For Kurelek, of course, had a different idea at the heart of his work: for him it was the Christian message that counted. Christ crucified appears dead centre in his *Dinnertime on the Prairies* (1963), and at front left in a tree in *In the Autumn of Life* (1964). Kurelek was at his best painting parables like *The Parable of the Sower* (1963), or the holocaust he fiercely expected, as in *And They Were Taken Unawares...* (1971) and *Not Going Back to Pick up a Cloak...* (1971). From first to last, his thoughts were on his message. In *Trustees Meeting on the Barber Farm, Regina* (1976), two pieces of wood on the ground form a cross. The initials Kurelek used to sign his work also featured a cross.

Emotional intensity is a keynote of his painting. Occasionally, he said, the painting took over and dictated to him, although this occurred only when he was under heavy pressure.[22] Things occurred then which he hadn't planned, and which pleased him. In a way, he needed the pressure.[23] It was "need"—the enthusiastic response of the public—which released in him the floodgates of his creativity, and proved always potent later in his life.

What salvages Kurelek's work for us today is not only his distant view—marvellously appropriate to landscape—but his curiously elusive details: the entrancing white horse gazing out from behind a silo in *Satan Sowing Weeds in the Church* (1963), or, in the same picture, the man in bed with his work-boots on the floor beside him, the garden by the house in *In the Autumn of Life*, the half-emerald, half-olive pine tree by the path in *Suburban Church* (1965), the houses on the horizon in his masterpiece *The Painter* (1974), the foreground weeds in *Abandoned Goulettes* (1976). After a while, you forget the clumsiness of Kurelek's way of painting and concentrate on surprises like these. On the other hand, sometimes Kurelek seemed possessed to put in *every* detail, like the police stopping a car in *Don Valley on a Grey Day* (1972). Occasionally a detail destroys a work, like the touch of scratched away snow in the background of *B.C. Seen through Sunglasses* (1973).

These examples of over-finishing suggest that picture making was like a game for him. Or perhaps Kurelek didn't know when to stop. Certainly his greatest difficulty lay in making his details combine with his abstracted backgrounds. Sometimes he managed it successfully, as in *Indian Summer on the Humber* (1972), light tonalities all the way through, *Plane Watchers at Malton*, and in part of *Newfie Jokes* (1974). (The rock in *Newfie Jokes* is an example of what did work: pencil dusted with colours.)

By the time Kurelek died, at fifty, he had just barely improved as a painter. The table-top composition remained, but by 1975 he could achieve small miracles of colour and mood (as in *Stooking*). A big show of his landscape paintings teaches you to hate the finicky detail and ever-present green grass. In his work, in fact, there's much to hate—an unformed sense of picture making, for instance.

But William Kurelek had a larger vision of Canada, and his struggle was not in vain. He contributed to Canadian art a special kind of awareness of what a symbol means. William Kurelek is the only Canadian artist who can, by showing us a path leading into the distance (as in his 1977 *Piotr Jarosz*), make us think of our impending death.

Notes
1. Joe Sornberger, "The Two Faces of Kurelek—Chronicler and Prophet," *Edmonton Journal*, October 30, 1976.
2. William Kurelek, *Someone with Me, The Autobiography of William Kurelek* (New York: Cornell University, Center for Improvement of Undergraduate Education, 1973), p. 31.
3. William Kurelek, *Kurelek's Canada* (Toronto: Pagurian Press, 1975), p. 12.
4. Metro Kurelek quoted by Peter Sypnowich, "The Easter Story," *The Star Weekly*, April 13, 1963.
5. William Kurelek, *The Passion of Christ* (Niagara Falls: Niagara Falls Art Gallery and Museum, 1975), p. 7.
6. "A Prairie Boy on Canvas," *Windsor Star*, October 16, 1975.
7. Videotape interview with William Kurelek by Phillip Earnshaw, Ray Konrad and Dell Wolfson, June 20, 1975.
8. Peter Sypnowich, "The Easter Story," *The Star Weekly*, April 13, 1963, p. 7.
9. Videotape interview with William Kurelek by Phillip Earnshaw, Ray Konrad and Dell Wolfson, June 20, 1975.
10. Foreword to *Nature, Poor Step-Dame* (Toronto: The Isaacs Gallery, 11–13 November, 1970), The Isaacs Gallery, Toronto.
11. *Kurelek's Canada*, p. 29.
12. Agnes McKenna, "Kurelek: Artist in Torment," *Oakville Journal Record*, February 13, 1976.
13. Marq de Villiers, "The Agony and the Ecstasy of William Kurelek," *Weekend Magazine*, July 6, 1974, p. 8.
14. *Someone with Me*, p. 448.
15. *Kurelek's Canada*, p. 88.
16. William Kurelek, *The Last of the Arctic* (Toronto: Pagurian Press, 1976), p. 14.
17. William Kurelek, *A Northern Nativity* (Montreal: Tundra Books, 1976), no. 6.
18. William Kurelek quoted by Judith Sandiford, "Painting beauty—Kurelek's 'miracle,'" *Ottawa Citizen*, March 6, 1976.
19. William Kurelek, *O Toronto* (Toronto: New Press, 1973), p. 32.
20. *Someone with Me*, p. 115; conversation with Jean Kurelek, February 24, 1982; videotape interview with William Kurelek by Phillip Earnshaw, Ray Konrad and Dell Wolfson, June 20, 1975.
21. *O Toronto*, p. 14.
22. *Someone with Me*, p. 238.
23. Marq de Villiers, "The Agony and the Ecstasy of William Kurelek," *Weekend Magazine*, July 6, 1974, p. 2.

Reminiscences
William Kurelek

In June when I first arrived in Toronto, I went around inquiring about the possibilities of starting a picture framing business. I also here and there inquired about the possibility of exhibiting my paintings. All galleries I tried had politely said "No, not interested," when I showed them my samples of paintings and frames. All, that is, except one—Av Isaacs who then had a shop on Bay and Hayter Streets. He got interested in my paintings mostly. "Could I see you later this year about the possibility of a show of your work?" he wanted to know. I agreed readily enough but couldn't believe he'd remember. I refused to raise my hopes.... Shortly after my getting down to work on the St. Matthew series the first break came. It was a short-term job of painting Av's gallery. He also said, "I'd give you picture frame work but I've not got it for the giving. However, if you make up some picture frame samples of real gold and silver work at my workshop, I'll see if I can get customers interested."

Thus, at first only a few hours, later a whole day, still later, two days a week, I began to work for him. I could now pay my rent. And here was sure proof of how God provides, for I had only about $15. of my savings left when this upswing of fortune began.... There were three men at Av's framing shop on Church and Front Streets, an unused warehouse, and Av kept contact with this shop from his Gallery by phone. The bright young foreman, Emmett Maddix, had just turned twenty. He started out along with Av when Av opened the business a few years previously. He had arrived just then in Toronto as an "immigrant" from Prince Edward Island. Then there was Stan Ross, a Belfast Irishman endlessly full of witticisms and gossip. He was a staunch Plymouth Brethren and as such, had no use for Catholicism at all. We two would get into theological debates, and Emmett, who was a lukewarm Catholic himself, would get exasperated. "Break it up you two. You should have been a minister and a priest." Frank Hislop was an old timer among picture framers in Toronto. I found out there was a popular history of that trade in the city and he knew it all....

Av and I got together enough of my paintings to form my first one-man show. A good third of them were loaned by relatives and friends. Not being able to sell, I had been giving works away. Finally came that fateful day. The show really and truly was put on! I was quite new to the procedure and rules of exhibiting. I found out about things like brochures, previews, newspaper reviews, refreshments, commissions, sales, reserves. In fact, Av gave me not one but two openings, the first for a Jewish women's organization. Thus ironically it was the Jewish Community who first discovered and patronized me, followed hard on by the Anglo-Saxons. The Ukrainian Community became seriously interested in my work about four years later. The show was an immediate success, both in sales, attendance and newspaper criticism, and my financial worries suddenly all vanished. I couldn't believe my eyes, ears or anything. I had a distinct feeling of unreality on those opening nights standing there in the crowds. "It can't be my pictures all these people have come to see—must be someone else's." It was the same a year or so later when Alfred Barr came from the Museum of Modern Art in New York and selected one of my paintings for his collection. The Art Gallery of Ontario sent a taxi to pick me up to meet him. That feeling of "it can't be true" took quite a few years to wear off because my successes became more fantastic. Eventually, my wife and I were invited to Prime Minister Pearson's residence for a State banquet because a painting of mine had been presented to Queen Elizabeth, the Queen Mother.

I'll never forget the time when at a show I had painted to honor my father, both he and Mrs. Pearson were present. I introduced him to Mrs. Pearson and they shook hands. "I never thought a great lady like her would pay attention to us" he confided to me later. It was a bit funny when he put his foot in it while conversing with her— "yes, I tried to raise my children well, and so I was concerned about the bad influences of Winnipeg when I sent them to school there." Mrs. Pearson was herself raised in Winnipeg where her father was a doctor. "Oh, I don't know about that," she replied, "my father was pretty strict with his children." To my big surprise my parents actually had come to my first show and have been coming ever since. At first they (mostly my mother) used to say of my successes—"It's alright—but will it last?" It was in 1967 that my father came right out and said he'd made a mistake about my vocation. This was after seeing me on television describing my early struggles. "I had no idea then what art was about, really," he said....

At first I fretted because I couldn't paint message paintings only. It wasn't that I didn't like doing the farm life ones. It was just that I felt a sense of urgency about the others. I'd discovered after the first two or so exhibits that there were these two main streams in my subject matter. I even made a special trip to Montreal to explore the galleries there, for I was looking for a specifically Christian gallery to represent me. I had a long talk about this dilemma of mine with Dr. Evan Turner, the Director of the Montreal Museum of Fine Arts, a man both Av Isaacs and I respected. It was evident by now, regardless whether I found it hard to believe or not, that my work had a permanent hold in at least the Canadian art scene. Dr. Turner advised me to give up the Christian Art Gallery idea. My best bet, he said, was to stay connected with Av Isaacs....

As I continued...I found myself called on more and more to speak before sympathetic groups and explain my art philosophy. Occasional harsh reviews of my religious art shows also had to be answered, I felt, so I began writing apologies. Av and I would have a collision on policy once in a while because of our different philoso-phies on art. It's never a serious collision, but sometimes calls for verbal clarification. As an example of these writings I will include here a talk I gave to a Ukrainian Literary Club in Toronto:

Before or after a successful show, journalists interview me or else I'm invited to speak before groups, or to appear on television, radio. I'm sometimes asked, or else forced by critics, to explain my philosophy of art. Art I find is a hard thing to define or pin down. Volumes of books have been written on it, but many of them don't seem to get down to the meat of it as far as I can gather from the few of them I've tried reading. I must confess, I'm rather skeptical about art discussions. That is why here, except for passing references, I'll not analyse other artists' work apart from my own. Frankly, there are some I just can't appreciate at all. For example, of all the big three, Michelangelo I'd say I do appreciate, da Vinci a little, Raphael just leaves me cold. On the other hand, Bosch or Redon or Corot or Goya really speak to me aesthetically. It's the same with music. Beethoven and Vivaldi yes, Mahler or Rachmaninoff nothing at all. I'd be rash to claim that Raphael or Mahler are not artists. What I will be explaining here therefore is just some of my conclusions about art. I arrived at them by personal experience rather than by study.

First of all, at the risk of shocking friends, I have to say I don't think art is the most important thing in life. People are. To be more specific, human souls. If there were thus a choice to be made—saving a person's soul or all my paintings, I wouldn't hesitate a moment in saying "destroy my paintings!" If there were a choice between the salvation of a man, even the lowest type, and the Mona Lisa, I'd say "burn the Louvre." (This is not the same as saving a person's life, as the question was raised in the film *The Third Man*. Everyone has to die sometime anyway.) Of course the above hypothetical point is that

I'm trying to say I feel art is today too often regarded as super-sacred and is worshipped almost like an impersonal god. Thus, some artists may lead loose lives arguing that since they're uninhibited by Christian ground rules they can drink life deep and so be more constructively creative. It still remains to be proven conclusively that lax morals do, in fact, increase man's creativity.

Then again "subject matter" in a painting tends to be regarded as dangerous by Modern Art worshippers for they say it stifles full creativity; at best it's only tolerated as a jumping-off point. Some critics really get at me because my subject often is story-telling or moralizing. But, you know, I do agree with them 100%. Subject is not what makes art. As a matter of fact, it's because I believe in the worthwhileness and value of art that I refuse to worry about whether I'm producing art or not. I don't think art is that delicate a creature. It's quite capable of taking care of itself. This is the marvelous thing, no matter what subject a real genius of an artist works on, art comes through it anyway. It's irrepressible. If God had given a man talent to produce art and his circumstances have instilled in him the drive to produce then he can't help but produce art if he paints or sculpts....

One of the amazing things about the Middle Ages... is that sculptors and painters were often anonymous. The perfect example of man giving glory to God really and truly can be seen in the sculptures that adorn the roofs of Gothic cathedrals. No one can possibly see the loving details of it way up there. Today however, artists sign their painting big and bold as if to say "I did it—all my own work—aren't I the greatest!" For a good while after my conversion I managed to put this conviction into practice myself by refusing to sign my paintings, or if I did sign them at the request of a customer, it was so hidden within the body of the painting that sometimes even I couldn't find it afterwards. Finally Mr. Isaacs forced me to compromise. Paintings were being sent back to Toronto by customers so I'd sign them and so prove they owned a genuine Kurelek. This compromise consisted of a monogram which I have designed, a W and K joined together with a little cross above it, and which I place in the lower right hand corner.

There is another wholesome and humble aspect of the medieval artist....It's that he wasn't so awfully conscious of art or of being an artist. In fact he merely thought of himself as a craftsman—in the case of a painter, for example, as a picture maker. Another craftsman would be a stonemason or a goldsmith or a tapestry weaver. So what it really meant was that a customer, usually the Church, but sometimes a wealthy townsman or noble, would ask for a picture. Usually it was of a particular subject, and the craftsman executed it for him to the best of his ability. It was just as simple as that. He had a shop like any other craftsman, employed assistants or apprentices or even his own family assisted him in the making of a picture....

Because that is the way I understand art, I have no hesitation in doing copies or similar pictures of my own work. Customers who missed out on buying an original of mine, either because it was already sold or it was too large, or too expensive, could still get what they wanted. The customer was happy. I was happy. My dealer, Mr. Isaacs, seemed to be the only one worried about the ethics of it— because of his purist philosophy of art. At the beginning of my showings at his gallery he also expressed concern because I was arranging my Ukrainian pioneer series of paintings in chronological order on his gallery. To him, the acme of aesthetic force is achieved when not only a picture stands unique in itself, but when the surroundings bow down to it too, as it were. Thus, such and such a picture looks best on that shape wall, or in that light, etc., etc., but what about the iconographer or the fresco painters like Giotto? They were paid to decorate certain pre-built architectural shapes and spaces. Not only that, but the subject was chosen for them. Did that stop their work from shining out as art masterpieces? Not at all!

Artists, or rather craftsmen as they thought of themselves, of those times did not lead esoteric personal lives either. Like solid tradesmen they haggled with customers over the price of their productions or services. They didn't look down on the "common herd." If their pictures sold well, then they lived as prosperous townsmen, married, raised a family. As I've said the sons often assisted their father in the craft of picture making, just as peasants' sons worked with theirs on the land....

I refuse to worry about whether I am producing art. I paint for a variety of reasons. One is to support my family. That's why every once in a while I take a field trip either to paint a particular locale or else to lock myself in a hotel in Montreal and paint memories of farm childhood. I turn out as many as three paintings a day working under an intense timetable of twelve to seventeen hours a day. These paintings I frankly call "pot-boilers." They are a saleable subject and size. Some buyers of these works are later offended if they overhear me refer to them as pot-boilers. It seems to imply that because they're churned out they're inferior in quality, in art. Not necessarily. They do have a comparatively more sketchy quality, true, but then so do the drawings and sketches of the Masters. Yet even the smallest thumbnail sketch of Rembrandt is chock-full of good art. Sometimes oddly enough, an artist working under pressure turns out some of his best work for the pressure tends to loosen him up.

Now to my religious works, which are didactic or moralizing. The subject is not dictated to me as it often was to medieval artists. I choose it myself and paint a theme that I strongly feel needs to be made public, and I deliberately use the popularity of my other more pleasant, memory-recording type painting so that I can attract the public. I've worked it out so that every second major exhibit of mine is moralizing, and every other one is merely story-telling. Eventually, perhaps these two main overall themes will become married, completely merged. For example, the large work I did which was purchased by the Canada Council entitled *Our World Today* shows what at first glance appears to be only a burning barn with children playing in it. But the title gives the clue (to me at least) as to why, with my particular vision of the moral decline of our evermore materialistic society, it would be dishonest for me to produce art for art's sake. In this vision I see the terrible consequences we will bring down on ourselves—total nuclear war and political tyranny.

In it most of our art may well be destroyed. "What's the use of painting beauty only, if this beauty will soon be destroyed?" I ask myself. The logical thing for me would be to turn to preaching the gospel of "repent and be saved," but if God had meant me to do strictly that, then He'd not have given me the talent to paint and draw. So all angles considered, it ends up that I'm doing exactly what I am supposed to be doing. Paintings may not have nearly the power to convert people that the printed or spoken word has, but each man has his part to play in the human and divine drama—some persons just a few lines, others whole pages. To refuse to play one's role at all is not the answer either. It is better to light one candle than to curse the darkness. In the divine economy nothing good that is done is ever lost. It may seem so for a while, but even to human eyes it can later turn up in a surprising way.

William Kurelek, *Someone with Me: The Autobiography of William Kurelek* (New York: Cornell University, Center for Improvement of Undergraduate Education, 1973), pp. 488–89, 496–98, 499–502, 503–5, 506–8.

List of Illustrations

Hauling Sheaves to the Threshing Machine 1961
Watercolour, ink, gouache, and oil on paper, 76.02 × 91.44 cm
C.I.L. Art Collection, Willowdale, Ontario

Threshing was the most exciting time of the year workwise. It was team work involving the whole family, neighbours and hired men. A double feeder machine required six racks to feed it and one or two field pitchers. Even the small children helped by spreading the grain in the granary, carrying lunch and water. The women cooked the big meals and looked after the farm yard. The owner had to be everywhere around the machine and tractor to see that it was in working order. In the picture we see him standing on top of the machine. It is four P.M. lunch time by the tractor. This is the only time of the year we had more than three meals a day. Work went forward from the time the dew dried up to well after dark.

Winter North of Winnipeg 1962
Mixed media on masonite, 101.60 × 127 cm
Hirshhorn Museum and Sculpture Garden,
Smithsonian Institution, Washington, D.C.

In this painting, I'm trying to convey the isolation of man in the vastness of the prairies, especially in winter when nature is particularly naked and merciless. Silhouetted on the horizon to the south is the lone rock escarpment on which Stoney Mountain Penitentiary was built. The boy on skis has ventured into the snowfields in a kind of instinctive dare against Nature and is now equally determinedly heading back for the security of the farm buildings.

The Atheist 1963
Oil and mixed media on masonite, 59.10 × 121.92 cm
Dr. W. Ellis, Elora, Ontario

Dinnertime on the Prairies 1963
Oil and mixed media on masonite, 72.14 × 44.27 cm
McMaster University, Hamilton, Ontario

The meaning of this picture is that our sins crucify Christ just
as much today, as 2,000 years ago, and just as much in Western
Canada, as in Palestine. The farmer and his sons doing the
fencing may have had an argument just before dinner or one of
them may have enjoyed a lustful thought. Or got an idea how
to revenge himself on neighbours, etc.

The Parable of the Sower 1963
Mixed media on masonite, 60.96 × 78.74 cm
James Richardson & Sons, Ltd.,
Winnipeg, Manitoba

Satan Sowing Weeds in the Church 1963
Mixed media on masonite, 60.96 × 78.74 cm
Ezio Cappadocia, Hamilton, Ontario

Another of Christ's parables in modern farm dress. The farmer's hired men, seeing weeds growing in a good field of wheat, ask their master if they should go and pull them up, but he tells them that an enemy maliciously sowed them while he slept and to leave them until the harvest, to be separated and burned. Otherwise, by pulling them up, they may disturb the not yet firmly rooted wheat plants. The field is the church; the enemy is the Devil, the weeds are bad church members; the wheat, the good members; the harvest, the Day of Judgement. As I see it, those of the Spanish Inquisition made the mistake of trying to root out bad members, and created a scandal which has lost the church more members than it saved.

In the Autumn of Life 1964
Oil on masonite, 59.10 × 120.30 cm
Art Gallery of Ontario, Toronto, Ontario
Gift of the McLean Foundation, 1964

(1) Atomic cloud, bursting over Hamilton, 14 miles from my father's farm, illustrated in this painting, is like a premonition of the disaster that will befall our materialistic society because it is so bent on pursuit of security and prestige, it ignores God. What I'm trying to say is that my father's life, hard as it may have been, is not a happy ending story, even though it may appear to be on the surface, judging by the large healthy family he has raised and the extent of his possessions. He will still have to meet "the day of Judgement." And Christ, whom he has ignored all his life, and maybe even helped crucify with his sins, is like a "skeleton" in his closet. It's an unpleasant scene, that he may try to keep off his property, but it's still there nevertheless.

(2) The dogs in the picture are "supernatural" ones referring to the enemies of Christ talked of in one of the Psalms of David.

Suburban Church 1965
Mixed media on masonite, 62.20 × 77.50 cm
Jewel C. McLeod, Hamilton, Ontario

And when Jesus came to the place, he looked up and said Zacchaeus, make haste and come down,
for I must stay at your house today. LUKE 19:5

This picture was done especially for Dr. N. B. McLeod, and the church is that of his former
congregation, St. Stephen's-on-the-Hill, Port Credit.

Flu Epidemic in Alberta 1966
Mixed media on masonite, 67.24 × 38.10 cm
Avrom Isaacs, Toronto, Ontario

This happened shortly after the First War. I recall
my mother talking of this and mentioning that all
went about wearing sterilized masks. When I
revisited the district 2 years ago doing research for
this project I dug up much more details. Some of it
was fanciful as for example that people dropped
dead all over like flies. But it was true that there
were so many funerals the custom of ringing the
church bells was dropped for the time being.
Another credible fact was the yellowy balmy still
atmosphere of the days that stretched out autumn to
past Christmas. The fancy came in again for
example when one woman averred this yellowness
was the mustard gas from the Western Front
trenches which had finally drifted in!

Lest We Repent 1966
Oil on pressed board, 68.58 × 53.34 cm
Agnes Etherington Art Centre,
Queen's University, Kingston, Ontario

This is of a scene I recall from early boyhood when I first began school. I knew this boy before he died of TB, for my brother and I sometimes played with him. I have shifted the season slightly from late fall to early winter, to better convey the impression of the once warm body going into the cold earth. The mother backed away from the mouth of the grave with a moan, as if crying, "No, no, no. It can't be true!" During our years of farming in that Manitoba district, there were several deaths in that family and yet the family, which was rather morally loose, turned over no "new leaf." This is the condition of our society generally today, which leaves it to the funeral parlour to disguise death as quickly and as quietly as possible, so as not to disturb anyone's state of mind or body.

Thanksgiving Day at Pohoolyanka 1966
Oil and pencil on masonite, 60.96 × 76.20 cm
University of Guelph Collection/Macdonald
Stewart Art Centre, Guelph, Ontario
Gift of Ayerst, McKenna & Harrison Ltd.,
Montreal, and the Alma Mater Fund, 1971

["Pohoolyanka" is a Polish word meaning "festive or dance place." This painting was
executed on the cottage lot of Kurelek's Polish friend, Roman Malanczak, on Lake Kaszube,
near Barry's Bay. Malanczak constructed the wayside shrine out of birch branches.]

36

Beauty and Peace: The Happy Family on Vacation 1968
Mixed media on masonite, 63.50 × 76.20 cm
Private Collection, Toronto, Ontario

◀ **The Devil's Wedding** 1967
Mixed media on masonite, 134.62 × 121.92 cm
James Richardson & Sons, Ltd.,
Winnipeg, Manitoba

Glimmering Tapers 'Round the Day's Dead Sanctities 1970
Mixed media on masonite, 121.92 × 243.84 cm
The Isaacs Gallery, Toronto, Ontario

In those Fall days when threshing would go on after dark there
might come a year or two in which the Northern Lights would
put on an awesome and entertaining show. I was surprised to
hear (and observe) when up in Cape Dorset that even at the
Arctic Circle the display is not as big and brilliant as farther
south, say around Churchill, Manitoba. I've shown them
dancing over our farm . . . no, "dancing" is not an accurate
word, nor is "glimmering" exactly on . . . "evanescing,"
perhaps. The long work day is over. Racks, teams, men clatter
on their way, farmyard bound, where a hearty supper waits.
The separator man moves the threshing machine to a safe fire
distance from the straw pile. By the light of gasoline lanterns
the owner and his boy scrape up the chaffy grain from the
ground, to save it for chicken or pig feed.

I Triumphed and I Saddened with All Weather 1970
Mixed media on masonite, 121.92 × 121.92 cm
Confederation Centre Art Gallery and
Museum, Charlottetown, P.E.I.
Gift of Noranda Mines Ltd., Toronto, Ontario

I've already described in my foreword the "message" of this picture and I mentioned that this is the one Ontario scene I've included. This is because the image left in my mind's eye of this one occasion on my father's farm near Vinemount fits this line of Thompson's so beautifully. Unlike the black earth of Manitoba, this Niagara gumbo soil is impervious to water, so that farmers here even have to make drainage ditches through their grain fields. In a heavy downpour, rain water collected in low areas to form a warm flood, and if that's where young grain stood it would turn yellow and rot. And what's more, some time after moving to his new farm Father was dismayed to discover that it lay across a watershed! I returned to Canada for a few months from England in 1956 and witnessed some of those heavy rains that summer. My father would be so glum, because he saw his income disappearing before his eyes. But the children—my young brother and sisters and their friends—were still too little to understand responsibility and economics, and so they donned swim suits and had a delightful sporting time charging across the fields with complete abandon. And though perhaps they weren't too conscious of it, they no doubt were excited by the natural drama of storm clouds and a rainbow above them as well as by the movement of water at their feet. In my own childhood, we children didn't dare show this enjoyment, as my father was driven by consuming ambitions in his younger days. I showed this in my painting *The Night the Barn Burned Down*, where my mother is shown scolding me for dancing with glee at the conflagration.

Thunder Driven 1970
Mixed media on masonite, 121.92 × 243.84 cm
Crown Life Canada Collection, Toronto, Ontario

Here is a memory of the drama Nature puts on often in the heat of a Prairie night. How well I remember lying awake on thundery nights, worrying that the lightning rods on our house wouldn't really work, that each flash of lightning might be followed by the crackling of burning shingles and ceiling boards. But until that night in wartime when there was no hired help I'd not had to meet that fury out in the open. My parents, driven by responsible husbandry, roused us at the unearthly hour of 2 A.M. to finish off a stack before an approaching rain cloud. Still aching-tired and half-asleep on our feet, we climbed on the stack. Father was already out there yelling and goading the horses on to extra speed. If the top of the stack was deluged while concave, the whole

of the hay, penetrated by moisture and encouraged by pressure and heat, would turn mouldy. And cows in winter turned their noses up at spoiled hay. Each lightning flash, like a wartime flare, would for an instant illuminate our work in harsh light, followed by the crackle-and-whomp of the thunder crash. And then the roll as the echo of it moved off, reverberating between cloud and earth. Each repeat of this performance galvanized us into an increased frenzy of work. We finished—we had to, however, make shift—and invariably arrived back at barn and house, both horses and men looking like drowned rats. Then back to bed, if there was still time.

40

Thy Young Skyey Blossoms 1970
Mixed media on masonite, 121.92 × 243.84 cm
The Isaacs Gallery, Toronto, Ontario

Firefly nights also, it seemed, came in one short period in the year in early summer. Like other things in nature, *e.g.*, rainbows, the pleasure and beauty of them is only in the beholding, or in anticipated capture, or even in pursuit after, but *not* in successful capture. For when we did cup one in our hands and brought it up to the kitchen lamp for examination, it proved to be only a nondescript ordinary little bug. Out there in the warm velvety darkness, however, their little lanterns winked at us teasingly again and so we still chased and gently captured them as if to show them we could. The firefly would glow like a coal off and on in our hands, a tiny spark fallen from the sun, left behind from the daytime. The tall trunks of the black poplars were like pillars in dark hallways of a palace ceilinged with garlands.

Ambush in Manitoba 1971
Mixed media on masonite, 78.74 × 116.84 cm
Michael Audain Collection, Vancouver, B.C.

Reprinted by permission of the
Pagurian Corporation Limited, Toronto:
from *Kurelek's Canada*.

And they were taken unawares, when the flood came and drowned them all; so it will be at the coming of the Son of Man. MATTHEW 24:39–40

The previous picture [Kurelek was referring to a painting in the show at which this picture was first exhibited], I discovered to my delight, led neatly into this one. Although the barn in the previous work is neighbour Peleshaty's and this one is our own, they could be interchangeable.

The previous picture in the series illustrated the text:

When the Son of Man comes all will be as it was in the days of Noah, in those days before the flood, they went on eating and drinking, marrying and giving in marriage, until the time when Noah entered the ark. MATTHEW 24:38

And They Were Taken Unawares...1971
Mixed media on masonite, 48.26 × 48.26 cm
Edmonton Art Gallery, Edmonton, Alberta
Gift of the Women's Society in memory of
Miss Mabel Grant, 1971

Not Going Back to Pick up a Cloak...1971
Mixed media on masonite, 48.26 × 48.26 cm
Avrom Isaacs, Toronto, Ontario

Not going back to pick up a cloak, if they are in the fields. MATTHEW 24:18

The next bomb falls on Winnipeg. One of us might be working on our
land across the bog road from the farmyard. Suppose he'd just hung his
coat up on a fence post because of the heat of the day...would he go back
for it, or would he make a dash *away* from the ominous mushroom shape?
Although horses have gone out of farm life, I brought them back into this
picture, as they better illustrate panic than a cold steel tractor would. They
are temporarily blinded. Otherwise they'd make a bolt for it too,
machinery and all. I know from experience how awful a "runaway" is.

44

Don Valley on a Grey Day 1972
Mixed media on masonite, 121.92 × 243.84 cm
The Isaacs Gallery, Toronto, Ontario

I got the inspiration for this painting from another artist, John Chambers. He did an enormous canvas of Highway 401 near London, Ontario. His clean-looking panorama made me want to do something like it as soon as I saw it at the Isaacs Gallery. I often use Bayview Avenue to visit my father-in-law in Sunnybrook Hospital, so I'm a good deal more acquainted with the Don Valley than the Humber. And despite all the signs and effects of industrialization impinging on it, it's still an impressive natural panorama when viewed from the Bloor Street Viaduct. I am in the picture, helping my two youngest children to enjoy the view. I'd all along intended doing the northward view. But on studying photos I took of both sides, I decided that the southerly view had more prospects compositionally. See if you can find the crucifix hidden in this painting.

William Kurelek, *O Toronto* (Don Mills, Ontario: General Publishing Co. Ltd., 1973), p. 6.

Indian Summer on the Humber 1972
Mixed media on masonite, 60.96 × 121.92 cm
Private Collection, Toronto, Ontario

The viewpoint of this painting is from a little man-made knoll on the east bank of the Humber River, near the Gardiner Expressway. The theme is that of the city basking for the last time in the serene glow of a warm, lazy autumn day. The leaves are already tinted and may even have begun to fall. Our streams are unfortunately too polluted for much in the way of fishing, but that doesn't stop the odd sportsman from trying. And, of course, early each spring there's smelt fishing at the mouth of the Humber.

Someone asked me if I had Thomas Eakins's picture of the sculler in mind when conceiving this painting. I must admit it did come to mind later while I was actually working on it.

William Kurelek, *O Toronto* (Don Mills, Ontario: General Publishing Co. Ltd., 1973), p. 20.

Opposite:
High Park was within walking distance when my wife and I settled in an Evelyn Avenue apartment in 1962. When I used to take our children to the small zoo there, I'd see excursion groups parading through. Many of them were school classes under the supervision of a teacher or two. No doubt their outing went under the subject of nature study or something like that. I didn't actually see this incident—the school group running for cover from a squall—but it provided a plausible story to go with my main artistic interest here, the dramatic effect of a sun-bathed hill-crest etched against a dark sky.

William Kurelek, *O Toronto* (Don Mills, Ontario: General Publishing Co. Ltd., 1973), p. 8.

Rainy Afternoon in High Park 1972
Mixed media on masonite, 76.20 × 81.28 cm
Private Collection, Vancouver, B.C.

◀ Plane Watchers at Malton 1972
Mixed media on masonite, 121.92 × 121.92 cm
The Isaacs Gallery, Toronto, Ontario

B.C. Seen through Sunglasses 1973
Mixed media on masonite, 31.80 × 78.74 cm
The Downstairs Gallery, Edmonton, Alberta

Opposite:

Somehow it seems the Toronto sky is most impressive in the west and northwest. Perhaps because that is where the sun sets, perhaps because that is where Toronto International Airport is located. Where there is aviation activity one looks up more often and is more aware of the sky. Twice, recently, driving to and from the airport, I spotted some plane watchers, so I added these as an essentially personal touch to go with the sky.

I use Toronto airport more and more, and appreciate the convenience of air travel. It's by plane that I can reach the Prairies for more inspiration related to my farm paintings. And from there I leave for other far parts of Canada with the intention of eventually making the whole country mine—the Arctic, the West Coast, the Maritimes. And abroad to Europe where my roots are, to Asia where the plight of the underdeveloped peoples cries out for compassionate comment. Yet always, at the end, the wheels of a jet touch down at Malton for me, for here is home base for me as an artist.

William Kurelek, *O Toronto* (Don Mills, Ontario: General Publishing Co. Ltd., 1973), p. 32.

This is again from one of those "happy accident" yellow-tinted slides. However this time it captures the sun-broken cloud formations so well, like all glory pouring down on earth, I decided to leave in the yellow cast and that's why the odd title. That's a lumber mill in the foreground.

A Ukrainian Canadian Prairie Tragedy 1974
Mixed media on masonite, 85.02 × 99.06 cm
The Isaacs Gallery, Toronto, Ontario

The Painter 1974
Mixed media on masonite, 121.92 × 91.44 cm
The Isaacs Gallery, Toronto, Ontario

To the outsider travelling through the prairies by train or car they seem monotonous and drab. I was lucky enough to have been born and raised there. So I can, I hope, see through to the beauty that arises from the many variations of interaction of sky and land divided by an uncompromising flat horizon. The prairies' crowning glory is without doubt their skies. Perhaps they're not as awesomely grand and varied as British Columbia's but they're panoramic nevertheless. When the weather forecast says scattered showers you can actually see several showers taking place within the full circle of your vision. Here I represent myself the happy artist recording this beauty as I did on a painting trip out West in my Volkswagen bug back in 1963. I lived, slept, ate and painted in the car. I recall one ecstatic evening in particular out on the bog to the east of our old farm. I photographed the skies all afternoon as well as making a series of water colors of them, until it was completely dark and the moon came out, at which time I was working by the car ceiling light. I still get a shiver of awe sometimes when I look at that series of photos in my album.

Reprinted by permission of the Pagurian Corporation Limited, Toronto: from *Kurelek's Canada.*

**◄ The Dream of Mayor Crombie
in the Glenstewart Ravine** 1974
Mixed media on masonite, 79.76 × 68.64 cm
Corporation of the City of Toronto,
Toronto, Ontario

When We Must Say Goodbye 1977
Mixed media on masonite, 19.68 × 91.44 cm
The Isaacs Gallery, Toronto, Ontario

Opposite:
On the whole as you see this painting has a fanciful, humorous, you might say light-hearted aspect. I resorted to a dream fantasy as a gimmick to incorporate many issues and ideals into one scene.... I find Mayor Crombie a very likeable person and I admire the idealism of his inaugural speech.... I was told recently that Mayor Crombie has the faculty of being able to roll with the punches. This has been proven to me by his accepting this painting. I was fully prepared to have it rejected on the grounds it was too controversial.

   Since it is going to stay, here is a run down of its details in case City Hall should want to pin the explanations beside the painting. I've shown the mayor on a grassy hillside which he is doing so much to keep green. This is beautiful Glenstewart Ravine which runs back of Balsam Avenue, my home street. Balsam Avenue, incidentally, appears as a snow scene on the cover of my book, *O Toronto*, published last year. In his hand is his inaugural speech which I was pleased to see printed on recycled paper. At his feet is a Protest march—garbage protesting his clean-up campaign. I've used artist's licence to replace the lovely homes on Glen Manor Drive across the ravine with a housing project for the underprivileged favoured by the mayor. That's him shaking hands with the builder. You'll notice the project blends with the natural setting. This is an integral part of the central slogan of his speech, "Renovate—Restore," towed by the helicopter labelled *The Greening of Toronto*. The mayor's accent on green is represented twice again in his planting of trees and more humorously spraying fresh green over pollution-soiled foliage.

Some one is said to have counted the mayor 19 times in the picture and the Mayor himself counted himself 14 times. When I heard this out of curiosity I counted too and found only 13 Crombies. In one place he's represented as an angel with white wings stopping smoke stack pollution. He's also firing warning shots at the air liner to keep quiet, but he's not seen behind.... Two places he is Superman—where he halts the Scarborough Expressway and stops the wrecker's truck. There's a little brook running down the centre of Glenstewart Ravine all year round. My small sons dump the frogs out in it they collect at my Dad's farm near Hamilton after studying them. That's the Mayor symbolically concerned over Toronto's natural water stream. That's him also showing his concern for Senior Citizens as he wheels and supports them by the brook wearing a halo. One of his projects which I was rather disappointed he gave up was cleaning up Yonge Street strip. I depict him being driven away from the job by critics accusing him of censorship. I also depict him closer to the front as re-elected mayor second time round because of his great popularity. And the glass pod stands for the Council Chamber here at City Hall in the centre of which he's represented as Big Chief Peacemaker. All these representations are allowed in a dream setting. All in all I painted this picture because Toronto is my adopted home and I love it and I'm glad Mr. Crombie is Mayor of this city because he obviously loves it too.

Excerpts from a talk given by William Kurelek, the text of which is in the City of Toronto archives.

Newfie Jokes 1974
Mixed media on masonite, 121.92 × 91.44 cm
M. M. Phillips, Toronto, Ontario

One of the joys of being human is the social pleasure of sharing a joke. A sense of humour is sometimes even a protective necessity. And I am sure that Newfoundlanders developed their peculiar view of humour, which all Canada now enjoys, as a comic relief to their difficult life in a rocky, misty land. Among those jokes are some dirty ones unfortunately. But I culled these out when I selected some fifteen for this painting. Apparently apart from being able to laugh at themselves there are four groups of people that are the butt of Newfie jokes: Nova Scotians, Frenchmen, Texans, and Torontonians. Typical of these are those on the craftiness of a Newfie "simpleton." Some are at the expense of the types of Toronto where Newfies often come seeking employment. You can read one such in the lower right-hand corner.

Reprinted by permission of the Pagurian Corporation Limited, Toronto: from *Kurelek's Canada*.

Pastoral Symphony 1974
Mixed media on masonite, 63.50 × 91.06 cm
Dr. J. H. Kawaguchi, Don Mills, Ontario

I'm afraid for the plausibility of this one. But I just had to do it. The scene is an authentic view of Prince Edward Island alright for it is an actual locale near Hunter River. And I saw plenty of such charming settings in my own travel through this "garden" province. The problem is that though it's possible that the two young hikers would be listening to Beethoven on their transistor radio it's hardly probable. It would most likely be Rock or Hank Snow or Stompin Tom Connors. And yet for me there just isn't any art as apt for the celebration of the beauty of P.E.I. country side except the music of the kind sensitive to daily or seasonal moods of nature as is Vivaldi's and Beethoven's. And for the artist in paints didn't Delacroix say that the first virtue of a painting should be that it be a feast for the eyes? What else can I add by way of excuse?

William Kurelek, *Kurelek's Canada* (Toronto: Pagurian Press, 1975), no. 10.

By The Breath of The Spirit II
1975
Mixed media on masonite,
101.60 × 71.12 cm
The Isaacs Gallery, Toronto,
Ontario

*The wind breathes where it will,
and thou canst hear the sound of it,
but knowest nothing of the way it
came or the way it goes; so it is,
when a man is born by the breath
of the spirit.* JOHN 3:8

**If God So Clothes the Grasses
That Tomorrow Go in the Oven**
1975
Mixed media on masonite,
101.60 × 76.12 cm
V. P. Boname, West Vancouver, B.C.

From the book *Fields* © 1976,
William Kurelek
published by Tundra Books.

No Grass Grows on the Beaten Path 1975
Mixed media on masonite,
101.60 × 71.12 cm
Avrom Isaacs, Toronto, Ontario

From the book *Fields* © 1976,
William Kurelek
published by Tundra Books.

Opposite:
[Stooking was one of the
harvesting operations before
combines came along and was
done by lesser persons, like girls,
extra youths and hired men.
Stooking allowed the wind to dry
the sheaves quickly and easily.
Also, if rain fell on them there
was much less chance of the heads
of the sheaves rotting or
sprouting.

In wet years there were more
mice than usual. They had to be
killed because of all the grain they
would eat. The running figure on
the right is attempting to catch a
mouse. While the mouse might
escape this time by hiding in the
next row, he would be caught
eventually when they stooked a
succeeding row.]

Paraphrased from William Kurelek,
A Prairie Boy's Summer (Montreal:
Tundra Books Inc., 1975), no. 17.

Stooking 1975
Mixed media on masonite, 35 × 35 cm
On permanent loan to the Art Gallery of Windsor,
Windsor, Ontario from Hiram Walker & Sons, Ltd.

Abandoned Goulettes 1976
Mixed media on masonite,
58.88 × 60.96 cm
The Isaacs Gallery, Toronto,
Ontario

This painting is meant to convey the sadness of a way of life that has passed. For over a hundred years these small timber transports plied the St. Lawrence River between the Saguenay and Quebec City carrying lumber and pulp logs to the mills at Quebec City. They were family boats. The mother was a cook, the father the captain, the children the sailors, and all lived on board during the shipping season. In winter the boats were winched up on to the land and stored on the dry dock rails you see in the foreground of the painting. Then new methods of transport, notably trucking spurred on by timber stands retreating inland, began to put these boats out of business. The last ones some of which Jim and I found at St. Joseph de la Rive were not even put in dry dock but simply dragged up on the beach to rot among the weeds. All the pictures in this series have people in them but I deliberately left people out of this picture to get across the idea of dereliction.

An Irish Settler's First Big P.E.I. Potato Harvest 1976
Mixed media on masonite, 60.96 × 121.92 cm
Bank of Nova Scotia Fine Art Collection, Toronto, Ontario

The Irish are known lovers of the potato since it was introduced into Europe from the North American Indians. The Irish were one of those peoples that brought it back to the New World. Today potatoes are Prince Edward Island's as well as New Brunswick's biggest items of export partly because the Irish as well as the French were the two main colonizing groups on that island. In the picture, one can see evidence of primitive agricultural practices. Many early settlers did not even understand the use of manure as fertilizer. Seaweed could have been used too as no part of P.E.I. is far from the sea. Even their cattle which grazed more or less freely in the clear forest areas would look stunted and bony compared to today's herds. P.E.I. pigs in the 1820s looked like greyhounds.

The soil of the island as I saw it is reddish. It was cultivated in between the stumps at first until many years later they rotted away. Only in the second generation did easily plowed fields appear and P.E.I. earned the name The Garden of Canada. As I've explained in the book done on my work embarrassingly titled *Kurelek's Canada* it was my visit to the Maddix family in P.E.I. that gave me an in-depth appreciation of the island more than a superficial bus or car tour would have done. Maddix is an Irish name, but the people on the island have intermarried so often now that French and Irish are hardly distinguishable. This marriage of the two races was facilitated, as it was in Quebec City for example, by the simple fact that both nationalities were staunchly Catholic.

The Marysville Cemetery 1976
Mixed media on masonite, 55.88 × 60.96 cm
The Isaacs Gallery, Toronto, Ontario

Father Kirley, French professor at University of Saskatchewan, introduced me to this subject. There were many solidly Irish settlements in Ontario, apart from the large numbers that chose life in the cities of Ottawa, Montreal, Toronto, London and Kingston. One such was in the district near Belleville, called Marysville. After the immigrants got through Grosse Isle or Montreal they fanned out into the new lands in the interior. They either used the travel route up the St. Lawrence and Lake Ontario, or the northern one via the Ottawa Valley. The northern one is full of Irish history. It was developed deliberately by the British, for despite its unattractiveness and poverty—it was a rockier, colder country—it was relatively safe from American conquest. Should Belleville, Kingston and Toronto which are just across the lake from the States fall, Canada could still have a lifeline through the north.

Father told me the suffering of the early Irish settlers could be almost literally read in the tombstones of Marysville Cemetery. I dropped in there one afternoon on the way home from our farm above Bancroft. It wasn't quite as simple as he implied. But if you studied the names, dates of death and ages of the dead on all the stones and put together the ones that died in the 1850s, you could see a pattern. I did this by taking many photographs and putting them together in this picture. The pattern bore out Father's statement that even after the potato famine refugees had made it to Canada, they continued to expire from the ravages of typhoid fever and malnutrition.

Smelt Fishing at St. Irene 1976
Mixed media on masonite, 55.88 × 71.12 cm
Price Waterhouse

A few years ago Vladimir was waked from his sleep in the dead of night by a neighbour. He urged him to hurry down to the St. Lawrence River as an extra heavy run of smelt fish had arrived on the beach at St. Irene about 8 miles away.

The sight that greeted him on that beach was incredible. There were hundreds of people there in the dark wading into the water to scoop up the fish that crowded together so thick there was no need to lure them. It was cold, there was still snow on the hills—so the men had to build bonfires on the beach from the plentiful driftwood. There they'd warm themselves and dry out their feet. A bottle was passing around for extra warmth and courage to venture back into the dark icy waters. It also encouraged a group camaraderie.

But beyond that it was a serious business. Each group while stoutly respecting the next group's little territory in the water was out to harvest a year's supply for their family's deep freeze. Every conceivable container and net was being used Vladimir noted and the catch was carried up to vans, pick-up trucks and car trunks. These vehicles were parked right up on the railway running between La Malbe and Quebec City fondly called "The Little Train." Everyone knew it ran only at certain hours in the daytime.

Trustees Meeting on the Barber Farm, Regina 1976
Mixed media on masonite, 60.96 × 121.92 cm
Dr. J. H. Kawaguchi, Don Mills, Ontario

Who Has Seen the Wind 1976 (1) ▶
Mixed media on masonite, 35.56 × 30.48 cm
The Downstairs Gallery, Edmonton, Alberta
Courtesy of Macmillan of Canada.

I have my three-quarters-Irish wife to thank for this picture. I was racking my skimpy ethnographic knowledge of Prairie history for some evidence of Irish settlement in Saskatchewan. I did in fact unearth one photo, one of the two at the National Archives in Ottawa. The caption on it said it was at the farm of Mr. Harry Boyle. That was not much help at all. At this point my wife reported that one of the members of her gym-and-swim class had relatives who had pioneered in the West. They were the Barber family, Protestant Irish who settled first near Orangeville after coming over from Ireland. The second generation however went much further afield: one to Australia, one to the North West Territories, another to Saskatchewan. My wife's friend even dug up old family letters written around 1890 to her mother back in Orangeville from her children in those far away places.

From old sepia photographs she also supplied, I reconstructed this farm scene just at the turn of the century at a place near Regina called Wolseley. There were cutters in front of the farm house though the snow was obviously already half melted. I imagined it might be a school Trustee's meeting at the very end of March. I figured if I put all the people in the house I could get across the courage of those early pioneering people in daring to set up home in what looked like the middle of nowhere. Those letters were revealing in this regard in that there is much talk of sickness and even death in them. They had a lot of privation in such isolation and mail came so infrequently because of great distances that misfortunes tended to be catalogued and compressed in communications.

◄ Who Has Seen the Wind 1976 (2)
Mixed media on masonite, 35.56 × 30.48 cm
The Downstairs Gallery, Edmonton, Alberta

Courtesy of Macmillan of Canada.

Who Has Seen the Wind 1976 (3)
Mixed media on masonite, 35.56 × 30.48 cm
The Downstairs Gallery, Edmonton, Alberta

Courtesy of Macmillan of Canada.

◄Who Has Seen the Wind 1976 (4)
Mixed media on masonite, 35.56 × 30.48 cm
The Downstairs Gallery, Edmonton, Alberta

Courtesy of Macmillan of Canada.

Who Has Seen the Wind 1976 (5)
Mixed media on masonite, 35.56 × 30.48 cm
The Downstairs Gallery, Edmonton, Alberta

Courtesy of Macmillan of Canada.

The Malanczak Summer Cottage 1977
Mixed media on masonite, 50.60 × 70.90 cm
Art Gallery of Hamilton, Hamilton, Ontario
Gift of the Polish Alliance of Canada and Wintario, 1978

I have known Roman for some twelve years now. First I used to give him rides to Madonna House . . . , which is not far from his cottage on Long Lake. Then I got my own farm studio near Madonna House so we're all set now to enjoy each other's company on the four-hour, 200-mile drive. His wife, Wanda, sometimes comes along. . . . Roman doesn't drive . . . so he comes up to his cottage (named Pohulanka after a district where he grew up in the Old Country) either by bus or with his children . . . or with me. I've included my car in the picture for compositional reasons, as they prepare to come back with me to Toronto. In many of my paintings I sneak Christian symbols into the composition. I didn't need to in a picture about Roman. He is a devout Catholic and isn't ashamed to show it.

Night Hunters 1977
Mixed media on masonite, 30.48 × 50.80 cm
Private Collection, Toronto, Ontario

The title of this series is derived from the slang term given the country of Canada, especially
Western Canada, by hobos and winos as they drift back and forth across the country
searching in vain for happiness, security, opportunity. . . . These lonely men have caught a
certain essence of this big land which at sometime or other, we all feel. It is that its enormity
dwarfs and dominates life, all life, both man and animal, whether it crawls, walks, or flies
over its surface, or tries to leave its marks on it such as dwelling places or modes of
travel. . . . Perhaps, I personally have experienced more of that than many of my urban-raised
compatriots, simply because I've been a loner since boyhood and have hoboed too across the
country. . . . But I've also tried to represent what other Canadians must feel about her. . . .
Night Hunters is an example of a disaster theme in which nature not only menaces, but has
the power to actually destroy or injure.

Piotr Jarosz 1977
Mixed media on masonite, 60.70 × 121.50 cm
Art Gallery of Hamilton, Hamilton, Ontario
Gift of the Polish Alliance of Canada and Wintario, 1978

This painting is deliberately the largest in the series [at a particular exhibition] as I've tried to convey some of the loneliness and harshness of homesteading in western Canada. We see Piotr Jarosz, an early homesteader, walking into Edmonton just barely visible on the horizon. I will paraphrase his memoirs:

> . . . I arrived in Edmonton in 1911 and found work in the city sewer system digging ditches. I was paid 10 cents an hour and worked there for two years. After I'd saved 60 dollars I bought myself a homestead at Rochester, 85 miles north of Edmonton. At the end of each month I walked there and back. My first house was a shack made of tree branches. The second house was still only one room but had a large fireplace in the middle of it.
>
> I still had to work outside to buy necessary tools and utensils for the farm and house.

Forewords
William Kurelek

On his Training

I have had little full dress art training; my colour, composition, method of paint application, etc. were arrived at mostly by intuitive groping rather than by systematic scientific enquiry and practice. In a word, I would not say I am a painter's painter. (1962)

On Childhood Memories

It should be noted that these are illustrations of *memories* and therefore they do not pretend to be accurate representations of the actual scenes. . . .

Since I am concerned with illustration, I feel I would like to get across to my viewers some facts about the scenes depicted—also to explain why this wish to deal with farm life. I believe I first became aware of it when I heard from my parents that my brother and I were to go to High School in the city. I remember how excited I was at the prospect of relating my farm adventures to the students I would meet. To my big disappointment, when we did find ourselves at school in the city, the situation turned out quite, quite differently. The city boys weren't in the slightest interested in country life, but seemed wrapped up in what seemed to me artificial concerns—the latest hit tunes, dating, movies, football games, etc. Some years later when two or three came down to the farm, they still didn't see the same things we saw, or not as deeply. By that time I had given up hope of getting this thing across and I little thought that it would persist and eventually, fifteen years later, find expression in this form—namely in my painting. I no longer really blame a predominantly urban Canadian public for failing to see or appreciate this particular communion of man with nature. It can't even all be put into pictures.

For instance—Spring in the West—I suppose it would need a poet to get across the thrill of the spring thaw in the West as we knew it; watching the giant snowbanks we'd become intimately acquainted with by playing on them during the long winter months, shrink and dwindle day by day. Not even country people we knew could be articulate about the vast chorus of frogs in the evening on the bogland to the east, or the swish of wild ducks' wings heard overhead before dawn while we did our morning chores. Going out to see flood waters running over sections of the farm at no other time flooded, would not be a city boy's idea of high adventure. But to me it was. (1962)

On his Sources of Inspiration

I realize religion is a touchy subject to a lot of people, and I suppose this is only natural since it reaches down to the very heart of every person—where he or she has more or less decided on the very purpose of life and what to do about it.

It would be easier for all concerned if I were a recognized master. For example, Rouault's "Miserere" etchings, an all-religious show at the Isaacs Gallery three years ago, was a decided success both in sales and in interest attracted. Rouault himself once said, "It is my hope that one day I will be able to paint a face of Christ so moving that anyone looking at it will be converted at once." I personally don't care for Rouault's style but I fully agree with that artistic aim of his. My conversion to Catholic Christianity six years ago is the best thing that ever happened to me and my dearest wish is to share my good fortune. This genuine desire to share is backed up with a sense of urgency too. It is rather as if I happened to be passing a neighbour's house in the country at night and I see it starting to burn. Instinctively, almost, I will rush over and try to wake the family by raising a commotion and then try to persuade them that the house is really on fire and to get out. This concern for the state of man's soul individually and collectively comes out in paintings. . . . I can't *help* but paint the sense of impending doom of our times; and the way of salvation too. I would be callous and dishonest if I buried my head in the sand. I am completely convinced that the Christian answer to life is the true one and being true, it cannot help but be organic. It is not as in the Soviet art, for example, where the artist is given a philosophical ideal to illustrate and tries to make the facts of nature fit into it. The trouble is that as soon as an artist gives way to the urge to get across a message, his work becomes didactic. And many people do not like being preached to. This is a centuries-old problem that painters and writers have grappled with, each in his own way....I am opposed to the *forcing* of ideals on others....Each man has a free will. I am presenting these pictures for everybody to look at, but I am *not* expecting everybody to accept the message in them, if they do not want to. I also am free. No church group has even suggested that I make such an exhibition. It is all my own idea.

Can a picture try to get across a message and still be art? I can vouch for it that I did experience the creative impulse while working on even the most didactic paintings....It would seem that subject matter cannot hold down a real genius, especially if he is given freedom to work on it in his native style. This is because art resides in *how* rather than in *what*. As my teacher Kimon Nikolaïdes said in his book *The Natural Way to Draw*—"It must not matter to the artist what subject matter temporarily proves convenient. The subject matter which is proper for you is that which gives you sufficient impulse to go on to a real creative effort. At the time when you are most interested in the act of painting, the subject will become entirely fused with the painting." This, I take it, means that even when the artist is *given* the subject matter, either by state, church or private individual, provided he can make it his own—that is, it excites his creative imagination in some way—it will be a work of art....For instance, if critics insisted that the artist must choose his own subject and the purpose for it, then they would strictly have to call Giotto an illustrator. He was given his subject matter—stories from the Bible which he had to depict on the walls of churches to *teach* the illiterate masses the Christian story. Suppose we consider the works of the great propagandists, moralisers, illustrators—Bosch's and Breugel's religious and social satire, *e.g.*, "The Seven Deadly Sins," which incidentally inspired my own *Seven Cardinal Virtues* series; Goya's *Horrors of War* etchings; Hogarth's *The Rake's Progress* paintings; Daumier's political satire cartoons; even Diego Rivera's communist murals—are these not regarded as works of art? I don't pretend to put my work on a level with theirs, but I nevertheless do have something to say, just as they did....

I should add that I mean to avoid offending any other religious group than mine, where possible. There has been quite enough religious strife in this sad world. Actually, only two or three paintings here could be labelled specially Catholic. The worst enemies of the Catholic Church are its bad members and natural error, although at the same time affirming that she is protected from failure by Divine promise. However, even if I am careful, sooner or later I am bound to offend some group or individual. That is the price of taking a definite stand on a serious matter. And I could go on and paint only nice, harmless pictures to serve the great god Art, which people will want to hang in their homes. But I would not be true to my inmost conviction and so I have to risk at least some loss of popularity and income, to paint these things that mean most to me. (1963)

On God

When I was a boy, my father used to quote a Ukrainian saying, "If you weep over the ills of the world, you will wash your eyes away." After I went out into the world I became aware of many of those ills besides my own, and I was bitter about man's follies and injustices, much as Jonathan Swift in *Gulliver's Travels*. Still later, after my conversion to the Catholic Christian faith, I became all the more conscious of this world as a "vale of tears." But now there was a significant difference. I know that God has the whole wide world in His hands and so good will triumph over evil in the end. It is the sins of men, and that includes mine (that's why I use we, our, us, in my titles) that blight the goodness and beauty of the world....

I know it sounds conceited to lecture my audience or to imply that I am endowed with some special understanding, but I find that I cannot harden myself according to my father's advice. Though I can clam up about my social concern in writing or in person-to-person conversation, it forces itself out in my paintings as surely as my farm subject-matter did because my city friends did not care to hear my country stories. (1966)

On Painting in the Arctic

I put on a heavy sheepskin coat and stretched two panels outside the back of the house. The first problem was painting the sun. It's hard to paint the sun, specially here, because if you look at it you get blinded and then when you return your eyes to the painting, there is this dark after-image of the sun dancing around on the board exactly wherever you put your brush down to paint. The glare is so strong, all the landscape—sky, as well as snowhills—are a blinding white and if I look through sun glasses the elements regain their distinction but then the colour values are knocked askew. Anyway, I kept slogging as I said with pale blues, whites, and touches of amber, ending up with an overall bomb-sprayed white in the sky. A black raven flying by added a vital touch of interest and below the mountain a Bombardier Tractor truck which I caught as it rolled down the trail....

Rendering ice is really tricky, I discovered, because its crystalline structure has so many hues and facets—like a diamond which you turn. But I worked and worked at it...until its form began to emerge strong with the help of spatter, wash, scrape, pencil and brush lines. I just

managed to complete it by dinnertime, and could relax at last, as I enjoyed the wine and juicy steak. (1968)

On the Last Days

I don't quarrel with the right of other artists to dedicate themselves to the search for pure artistic expression; I myself couldn't honestly do the same. This is because our age is one of deep moral crisis, and following on that— great physical danger....(1969)

"Vision" is the only word I can find to name that intuitive premonition of what the modern world is heading for. It's not only that the signs are there for most persons to see. We all know that the nuclear weapons stockpiles are very real. And those bombs have already been used on human beings. But what of the increase of violence, the rapid erosion of legitimate authority, the increasing poverty of the have-not nations coupled with the "last-days-of-the-Roman-Empire" kind of moral decay of the affluent West? All these point to some kind of explosion. Intuition and vision have ever been legitimate sources of creativity for the poet and the painter. And now it is for the film-maker too, it seems. Even if the vision is manic, as in the works of Goya, Bosch, Bacon and others, the world accepts their right to the expression of it.... Pictures are democratic. If there is a sermon contained in them it can be taken along or left behind when the viewer leaves the gallery. (1971)

About Nature

Nature gives not a drop of comfort, can do nothing, will do nothing. She existed millions of years before human beings with feelings appeared on the scene. And just as then, so today living beings are trapped by her pitiless laws....

Most of my works thus far have been of a portable under-the-arm size because I work not on an easel but on a table. The single outstanding feature of prairie landscape, however, just as of the ocean, is *expanse*. And I figured if I kept my human figures their usual size but increased the area of the painting itself, the end effect would, by sheer contrast, be expansive. And in that expanse are liberally laid out the basic elements of soil, sky, cloud, wind, grass, poplar bush, snow and sun.

On the other hand, I've also included rare natural phenomena so that...I could prove I've not misjudged Mother Nature and called her poor before really experiencing everything she had to offer. Northern lights at their most spectacular come only in cycles of years, an eclipse of the sun is a twice-in-a-lifetime event, firefly nights are a few in the late spring or summer, snowball weather is about a week at the tail end of winter on the Prairies....

[But it's important to realize that] nature's display of beauty—for example, in the rainbow—is just so much mockery to the farmer whose crops she has flooded out....

Dressing the message in authentic clothing is still my particular painter's problem. (1970)

The Gospel according to St. Matthew

I had begun back in 1959 with the six-year labour on the Passion according to St. Matthew. Christ used the later destruction of Jerusalem by the Romans and the dispersing of the Jewish people in 70–73 A.D. (an event He accurately prophesied) as an example of the end of the world. Actually this coincides with my concept of the sequence of events. Since the events I'm portraying are of the future, I decided it was useless trying to imagine the actual appearances of things like clothes, scenery, or machines, for that would be dating it all and making me an Adventist. So just as other artists (notably Stanley Spencer) have used their own time, locale, and personal experiences to illustrate the past and future described in the Bible, I decided to draw on my past experiences on the

farm in Manitoba where possible. Probably the people of the Stonewall district would be amused to see the countryside they know so well used as a backdrop for such momentous and dramatic occurrences (actually the cities will be the ones to suffer most in the last days). But in considering my audience I knew that the countryside always has more eye-catching appeal than a cityscape. (1971)

On Toronto

I first became acquainted with Toronto back in 1949, the year I graduated from University of Manitoba and decided to move east to enter the Ontario College of Art. By coincidence the rest of the Kurelek family had decided to move that same year to the less harsh climate of the Niagara Peninsula.

It was commonplace at that time to assess Toronto as being cold and unfriendly. And my first experiences here were bitter and unhappy too....But by a strange alchemy there took place something akin to the common plot of Harlequin romances. The hero or heroine ends up falling for the very person they first hate or fear. By the time I decided to go abroad a year later, I realized that I had actually come around to liking this city. I remember promising myself at my departure that if I ever came back to settle in Canada, it would be in Toronto. Nine years later I kept that promise. (1972)

On Machines

To me, man is more important than machines. But on the other hand man was given the divine commission to subdue the earth and make it his. (1973)

On Artistic Expression

...Progress for most artists results from their effective struggle to solve problems of artistic expression. Usually it's a stylistic or technical one. My main problem, on the other hand, has been and still is one of getting across a message. Sometimes, frankly, I try to do it by dressing it up in the clothing of a pleasant pastoral scene. Or if it's a series of paintings I try to strike a publicly acceptable balance between beauty and message. The trouble is, many of these messages...are so strong that they overpower even a deliberately pleasant series....(1974)

On the Passage of Time

Some regard me as the only pictorial chronicler of the immigrant pioneer tamers of the Canadian prairies. As if for that reason I was born of those very people forty-seven years ago in the Willingdon-Vegreville district of Alberta. Not only that, I came in, as it were, with one foot in the end of the pioneer era, and one in this present technological era. This technology makes it possible to raise a country's wealth, education and communications to the point where, within a few years, works of art can be conceived, executed, bought and then circulated to help raise the cultural level of a whole country....

An indication of the amazing rate of change in prairie farm life...is the fact that my grandfather, who came to Canada from the Ukraine before the First War, worked together with his father to break and work the virgin soil—with oxen! Even my father still remembers seeing the steam engines, "the gentle giants of the plains"..., threshing and soil-breaking. But I don't. I, myself, worked the land with both gasoline tractors and horses and I paint my experiences with these. But already my pictures of farm horses are being bought for their nostalgic value by Westerners who live in Toronto or Montreal, because one no longer sees horses on the land....

I just wish it were allowed for me to do about six weeks of on-the-spot work in the fascinating village from which my family emigrated to Alberta. I was allowed four hours there on my trip to the Ukraine in June of 1969—a mere fleeting glimpse of the faith and industry at my people's roots. No way will the Soviet regime allow me such a painting trip. With it I'm sure I could bridge the gap between my cultural and social roots over there and the free climate of artistic expression enjoyed here by the various ethnic groups in Canada. (1974)

On Canada

Willy-nilly I seem to have acquired a reputation as a painter of Canadiana, or rather as a recorder of Canadian prairie life in particular. It occurred to me therefore that if I could widen that subject matter by depicting all Canada to all Canadians I would then be in a position to reach all the more people with my messages too....The motive is double barrelled. Somewhat like the Newfie who loaded one barrel of his shotgun with shot to kill the bird and the other with salt to preserve it till he finds it....To that end I've been making each of my painting trips in the past two years to a different province. I didn't actually paint that particular province at that time. But just being there already assured me of at least a nodding acquaintance with that part of Canada....

I don't consider Canadian citizenship nearly as important as citizenship in the Kingdom of Heaven. After all, each Canadian citizen is that for only a brief span of seventy years, but a citizen of the next world forever. At the same time, however, I am proud of being a Canadian, just as I am of my Ukrainian ancestry. And I truly love this country. There was a time during my boyhood in Manitoba—I used to feel the call of the great, free, flat bogland to the east of our farm. I found myself walking or cycling out on it whenever freed from farm work. Even though my father didn't actually own a single foot of it, it still said to me, "You and I belong to each other." When I grew up I travelled in many countries and even became so fond of England during my seven-year stay there that I almost remained. But Canada eventually won. And despite the disturbing things I see hurting her, which I will continue to protest, I am happy to be home. (1974)

Sources of Inspiration and Medium

I paint from within mostly, so it doesn't matter when or where I am while producing. The medium is called mixed, something I developed myself over the years....It is predominantly oil, but there is also lacquer, graphite, coloured pencil and pen-and-ink on a gesso base which I scratch through in places where I need a fine white line. Even though the paintings were done in one fell swoop I kept polishing them now and then for a few months after. (1975)

The Irish in Canada

Since the time I first began...recording the history of the major ethnic groups in Canada, I knew there was no way I could miss the ubiquitous Irish. At one time...they were the largest pioneering group here, next to the French. And they came early. There are Irish enclaves in Newfoundland, for example, still speaking a Gaelic brogue that dates back four hundred years.

The Irish, as everyone knows, are quite conscious of their background. Their folk songs speak of their love for the "Emerald Isle." Why then did they leave in such numbers? It was plainly dire necessity—poverty and oppression. In fact, the Irish resemble the Ukrainians in several ways. They both have a long history of foreign subjugation and, as a result, are nationalistic. Both have suffered much and have been visited by calamities. Both have had a golden age in their history. Both have a love of singing and, in fact, have produced heart-stirring folk songs. Both have been forced to emigrate. The Irish have been more successful, however, in leaving their mark on North America because they came earlier, in larger numbers, and already spoke the English language....

As an historical painter...I had to record the crises, the calamities, the hunger, thirst, sweat, toil of the people settling into an untamed country. This I feel is nothing to be ashamed of. On the contrary, it glorifies the courage, the service, the toughness of this race....In each of my ethnic series, I find it hard to convince the particular group that this is important or that I'm serious about doing it. (1976)

On the Canadian Landscape

"Big Lonely" is the slang term given the country of Canada, especially Western Canada, by hobos and winos as they drift back and forth across the country searching in vain for happiness, security, opportunity....

...These lonely men have caught a certain essence of this big land which at sometime or other we all feel. It is that its enormity dwarfs and dominates life, all life, both man and animal, whether it crawls, walks, or flies over its surface, or tries to leave its mark on it such as dwelling places or modes of travel. There is an obvious contrast in this respect between our country and Europe, for example, where man over thousands of years has come to dominate nature, in fact, to nearly completely subdue her, except in a few areas, such as the Swiss Alps, or the Russian Taiga. One has only to consider the stark fact that Canada's population is a mere thin ribbon stretching across the continent just above the American border.

Perhaps, I personally have experienced more of that than many of my urban-raised compatriots, simply because I've been a loner since boyhood and have hoboed too across the country....

A Yukon trapper must feel a special warmth towards his little cabin stops, after a long day checking his trap lines. A snowplow man must wonder sometime during a really bad winter, whether it will beat him or he it. Most Canadians, in the not so distant past, used to feel the haunting loneliness in the sound of a ship's foghorn as it left for distant lands or the whistle of a freight train as it echoed in the mountain valleys. (1977)

Select Bibliography

Primary

Kurelek, W. *Fields.* Montreal: Tundra Books Inc., 1976.

———. *Fox Mykyta.* Montreal: Tundra Books Inc., 1978.

———. *Kurelek Country.* Boston: Houghton Mifflin Company, 1975.

———. *Kurelek's Canada.* Toronto: Pagurian Press, 1975.

———. *The Last of the Arctic.* Toronto: McGraw-Hill Ryerson, 1976.

———. *Lumberjack.* Montreal: Tundra Books Inc., 1974.

———. *A Northern Nativity.* Montreal: Tundra Books Inc., 1976.

———. *O Toronto.* Don Mills, Ontario: General Publishing Co. Limited, 1973.

———. *The Passion of Christ According to St. Matthew.* Niagara Falls, Ontario: Niagara Falls Art Gallery and Museum, 1975.

———. *The Polish Canadians.* Montreal: Tundra Books Inc., 1981.

———. *A Prairie Boy's Summer.* Montreal: Tundra Books Inc., 1975.

———. *A Prairie Boy's Winter.* Montreal: Tundra Books Inc., 1973.

———. *Someone with Me: The Autobiography of William Kurelek.* Ithaca, New York: Cornell University, Center for Improvement of Undergraduate Education, 1973 (out of print); Toronto: McClelland and Stewart, 1980.

———. *The Ukrainian Pioneer.* Niagara Falls, Ontario: Niagara Falls Art Gallery and Museum, 1980.

Kurelek, W. and A. Arnold. *Jewish Life in Canada.* Edmonton: Hurtig Publishers, 1976.

Mitchell, W. O. *Who Has Seen the Wind.* Toronto: Macmillan of Canada, 1975.

Nicolaïdes, K. *The Natural Way to Draw.* Boston: Houghton Mifflin Company, 1941.

Paximadis, M. *Look Who's Coming: The Wachna Story.* Oshawa: Maracle Press Limited, 1976.

Secondary

Anon. *William Kurelek.* Art Gallery of Brant, Brantford, Ontario: Exhibition Catalogue, May 3–26, 1974.

Ayre, J. "The World of William Kurelek." *Saturday Night,* April 1974.

Ayre, R. "Kurelek—Memories of Manitoba." *Montreal Star,* July 15, 1967.

———. "Probing Lasting Values." *Montreal Star,* August 30, 1969, p. 14.

Bacque, J. "Kurelek's Toronto: A Unique and Gripping Vision." *Toronto Life,* November 1973.

Bell, P. "Paintings Exhibit Extraordinary Understanding of Composition." *St. John's Evening Telegram,* March 1, 1980.

Cook R. "William Kurelek: A Prairie Boy's Visions." *Journal of Ukrainian Studies* 5 (Spring 1980), pp. 33–48.

Dault, G. M. "Kurelek's Quality Undermined." *Toronto Star,* November 24, 1976.

———. "One Man's Joy in the Big Land." *Books in Canada,* November 1975.

De Marco, D. "Kurelek: Artist or Propagandist?" *Chelsea Journal 1* (Saskatoon) (March/April 1975), pp. 81–84.

———. "William Kurelek: Message Painter." *Uncertified Human 5* (Toronto) (February 1978), pp. 3–7.

De Villiers, M. "The Agony and the Ecstasy of William Kurelek." *Globe and Mail,* Weekend Magazine, July 6, 1974, pp. 2–8.

Edmonstone, W. "Ora Pro Nobis, William Kurelek." *Vancouver Sun,* November 5, 1977.

Fulford, R. "Bill Kurelek Remains a Stranger Despite the Success of His Art." *Toronto Star,* December 8, 1973; printed concurrently in the *Ottawa Citizen;* reprinted in *Promin* 15 (March 1974), pp. 13–15, 18, with comment by William Kurelek.

Jarmicki, E. "The Metier of Kurelek." *Canadian Register* (Kingston, Ontario), December 9, 1961.

Kilbourn, E. "W. Kurelek." *Canadian Art 78* (March/April 1962), pp. 136–37.

Lanthier, P. "The Artist as Piers Plowman." *Matrix* (Champlain College), Fall 1975.

Legge, E. and S. Madill. *Kurelek.* Winnipeg Art Gallery: Exhibition Catalogue, October 10–November 23, 1980.

Lowndes, J. "Kurelek: Visionary Painter As Pragmatic Salesman." *Vancouver Sun,* October 13, 1973.

Michener, W. "Kurelek." *Globe and Mail*, Weekend Magazine, January 20, 1968.

Nixon. V. "Kurelek's Message Is Sharp and Clear." *Montreal Gazette*, June 19, 1971, p. 43.

Oxorn, P. "Kurelek Captures Christian Message." *Ottawa Journal*, March 3, 1977.

Purdie, J. "People's Painter Depicted Canadian Life, Religious Themes." *Globe and Mail*, November 5, 1977.

Richmond, J. "The Light from Hidden Icons." *Montreal Star*, November 3, 1974.

Russell, P. "Masterpieces from the Prairies' Painter." *Toronto Daily Star*, November 14, 1970.

Sandiford, J. "Painting Beauty Kurelek's 'Miracle'." *Ottawa Citizen*, March 6, 1976, p. 72.

Tyrwhitt, J. "William Kurelek: The Power of Obsession." *Saturday Night*, May 26, 1962.